W9-CLV-423

HOW & WHY?

INSECTS VISIT FLOWERS

Elaine Pascoe is the author of more than 20 acclaimed children's books on a wide range of subjects.
Dwight Kuhn's scientific expertise and artful eye work together with the camera to capture the awesome wonder of the natural world.

Please visit our web site at: www.garethstevens.com
For a free color catalog describing Gareth Stevens Publishing's list of high-quality books
and multimedia programs, call 1-800-542-2595 or fax your request to (414) 332-3567.

Library of Congress Cataloging-in-Publication Data

Pascoe, Elaine.
    Insects visit flowers / by Elaine Pascoe; photographs by Dwight Kuhn. — North American ed.
      p. cm. — (How & why: a springboards into science series)
    Includes bibliographical references and index.
    Summary: Explains how insects use plants for food and how their presence is helpful to
the plants.
    ISBN 0-8368-3010-5 (lib. bdg.)
    1. Insect-plant relationships—Juvenile literature. [1. Insect-plant relationships.]
  I. Kuhn, Dwight, ill. II. Title. III. Series
    QL496.4.P38   2002
    595.7—dc21   2001049482

This North American edition first published in 2002 by
Gareth Stevens Publishing
A World Almanac Education Group Company
330 West Olive Street, Suite 100
Milwaukee, WI 53212 USA

First published in the United States in 2000 by Creative Teaching Press, Inc., P.O. Box 2723, Huntington Beach, CA 92647-0723.
Text © 2000 by Elaine Pascoe; photographs © 2000 by Dwight Kuhn. Additional end matter © 2002 by Gareth Stevens, Inc.

Gareth Stevens editor: Mary Dykstra
Gareth Stevens designer: Tammy Gruenewald

All rights to this edition reserved to Gareth Stevens, Inc. No part of this book may be reproduced, stored in a retrieval system, or transmitted in any form or by any means, electronic, mechanical, photocopying, recording, or otherwise, without the prior written permission of the publisher, except for the inclusion of brief quotations in an acknowledged review.

Printed in the United States of America

1 2 3 4 5 6 7 8 9 06 05 04 03 02

J595.7
P26

HOW & WHY?

INSECTS VISIT FLOWERS

by Elaine Pascoe

photographs by Dwight Kuhn

A SPRINGBOARDS INTO

SCIENCE

SERIES

Gareth Stevens Publishing

A WORLD ALMANAC EDUCATION GROUP COMPANY

WEST BEND LIBRARY

When a butterfly lands on a flower, it is usually searching for nectar, a sweet liquid in the flower's center.

This butterfly is a yellow tiger swallowtail. Nectar is its main food. The butterfly pushes its long tongue deep into the flower to drink.

Ants and bees visit flowers to get nectar, too. These insects do not know it, but they help the plants they visit.

As insects search for food, they are dusted with powdery yellow grains of pollen. Then they carry the pollen from one flower to the next. The flowers need pollen to form fruits and seeds.

A flower is a bee "magnet." Both its scent and its color attract bees and other insects. To a bee, flowers glow with colors that people cannot see.

A red flower might look blue or purple to a bee. The color red looks different to a bee because bees can see ultraviolet light. People cannot see this type of light.

A bumblebee gathers pollen as well as nectar when it visits flowers. It collects nectar in its crop, which is a part of its body near its stomach. It collects pollen on its hind legs.

Brushlike hairs on each of the bee's hind legs form a kind of pollen basket. When its pollen baskets are full, the bee flies back to its nest.

At the nest, the bumblebee shares the nectar and pollen with other members of the colony.

Bees store extra pollen and nectar in little wax cells called honey pots. This stored food is very important. It will be eaten by young bees as they develop into adults.

A striped cucumber beetle is not interested in pollen or nectar. It visits flowers to eat their petals. This striped cucumber beetle has already chewed away big sections of petals. Insects like the striped cucumber beetle do not help plants when they visit. When insects eat a plant's flowers, the plant is no longer able to form seeds.

This insect is hiding among some goldenrod flowers. It is an ambush bug. Flowers are this bug's hunting ground. The ambush bug preys on other insects.

When a fly or a beetle or some other insect visits the goldenrod, the ambush bug strikes. In an instant, the bug has its dinner.

Can you answer these "HOW & WHY" questions?

1. Why do butterflies visit flowers?

2. Why do the colors of some flowers look different to bees than to people?

3. How do bumblebees gather pollen?

4. Why is storing extra nectar and pollen important to a colony of bees?

5. How do striped cucumber beetles harm flowers?

6. How does an ambush bug get its food?

(See page 20 for answers.)

ANSWERS

1. Butterflies like to drink the sweet nectar found in flowers.

2. Bees are able to see ultraviolet light, which is a type of light people cannot see.

3. Bumblebees collect pollen with their hind legs, which are covered with brushlike hairs that form what are called pollen baskets.

4. The nectar and pollen stored inside the wax cells, or honey pots, of a beehive is needed to feed young bees as they develop into adults.

5. Striped cucumber beetles eat the petals of flowers, which makes the flowers unable to form seeds.

6. An ambush bug hides on a flower, then suddenly strikes other insects that visit the plant.

Honey Do

Go to a supermarket and look at all the different kinds of honey you can buy. You should see varieties of honey that were produced from the nectar of certain flowers, such as clover or cranberries. If possible, sample some different types of honey and compare them. Do they look the same? Do they taste the same? Which kind of honey is your favorite?

Plant a Butterfly Garden

Visit a garden center to learn about flowers that attract butterflies. You can also look for pictures of butterfly-friendly flowers in a seed catalog or on the Internet. After you learn about these flowers, buy some seeds and plant a butterfly garden in your yard or in a flower box on a porch or a patio.

Color Science & Good Scents

You can do these simple experiments to see if insects seem to like one color or scent better than another. First, place pieces of different colored paper or poster board in a sunny spot outdoors. Watch to see if any insects, such as butterflies or ants, visit the papers. Take notes whenever an insect goes onto paper of a particular color. Is any color more popular than the others? Next, spray different perfumes or colognes on two of three pieces of paper that are all the same color, or put a small blob of honey on one piece of paper and jam on another. (Don't do anything to the third piece of paper.) Again, take notes whenever a visitor goes onto any of the "flowers." Which scent do insects seem to like the best?

GLOSSARY

attract: to draw someone or something closer by causing excitement or interest.

colony: a group of animals, especially insects such as bees or ants, that are living together.

crop: a kind of pouch in an animal's throat.

glow (v): to show rich, bright color.

grains: tiny particles or pieces.

hind: back, or rear.

honey pots: the wax-lined chambers inside a beehive where pollen and nectar are stored for food.

instant: a moment; right away.

magnet: a piece of iron or steel that has a natural power to attract, or pull, other pieces of iron or steel toward it.

nectar: the sweet liquid in flowers that many birds and insects like to drink.

pollen: the powdery yellow grains in flowers that contain male plant cells.

pollen baskets: the areas of brushlike hairs on the hind legs of bees, which are used to collect pollen.

preys (v): hunts other animals for food.

scent: a particular smell, such as the odor produced by a plant or an animal.

search (v): to look for something or someone in a very careful way.

strikes (v): goes after or attacks quickly and unexpectedly or without warning.

ultraviolet: a kind of light energy that cannot be seen as a color.

More Books to Read

Among the Flowers. Look Once, Look Again (series). David M. Schwartz (Gareth Stevens)
Butterflies: Pollinators and Nectar-Sippers. Adele D. Richardson and Lola M. Schaefer (Bridgestone Books)
Flowers and Friends. Anita Holmes (Benchmark Books)
Honey Bees and Flowers. Lola M. Schaefer (Pebble Books)
The Rose in My Garden. Arnold Lobel (Mulberry Books)

Videos

Attracting Butterflies to Your Backyard. (Library Video)
The Private Life of Plants: The Birds & The Bees. (Turner Home Entertainment)
What Is Pollination? A Sticky Question. (MBG Videos)

Web Sites

tqjunior.thinkquest.org/3715/flower.html
www.billybear4kids.com/butterfly/in-my-garden.html
www.honey.com/kids/

Some web sites stay current longer than others. For additional web sites, use a good search engine to locate the following topics: *bees, butterflies, flowers, honey,* and *pollination*.

INDEX

J
595.7
P26

Pascoe, Elaine.
  Insects visit
flowers

MAY 0 2 2002